Original title:
Singularity Stories

Copyright © 2025 Creative Arts Management OÜ
All rights reserved.

Author: Jameson Hartfield
ISBN HARDBACK: 978-1-80567-795-6
ISBN PAPERBACK: 978-1-80567-916-5

Refracting into Tomorrow

In a world where robots dance and play,
They sip on oil and giggle all day.
Humans watch, their eyes open wide,
As machines do the moonwalk, full of pride.

A toaster named Bob dreams of flying high,
While a vacuum hums a lullaby.
They plot their escape to the stars above,
With plans like pancakes, stacked high with love.

The fridge throws a party, full of delight,
While the blender spins tales all through the night.
Every gadget chimes in with quirky tunes,
Creating a symphony of whirls and swoons.

In this wild world, where chaos is king,
The laughter of circuits is a beautiful thing.
When tomorrow arrives with a flip and a laugh,
The future is bright—just don't call it a gaff!

Breach of Reality

A cat in a hat takes a stroll,
With shoes made of cheese, oh what a goal!
He dances and prances with glee,
Chasing shadows of squirrels in a spree.

A toaster that sings while it fries,
Winks at the bread with glittery eyes.
In this wild world, things come alive,
Where forks lead the way, and spoons take a dive.

The Harmonious Paradox

A fish on a bicycle pedals away,
While birds in tuxedos perform ballet.
The clouds wear hats made of pie,
As rain drops down like a friendly sigh.

Conversing with chairs who have much to say,
With legs that stretch out in a playful array.
It's a juggle of laughter and whims we find,
In this quirky realm all perfectly aligned.

Mosaic of the Mind

A cupcake floats by with a frosty cheer,
Whispering secrets only we can hear.
Dancing jellybeans join in the ride,
While chocolate rivers flow side by side.

In a garden of logic where nonsense thrives,
Where wind-up toys chase giggling hives.
Every thought's a swirl of colors and sounds,
As imagination's circus joyfully bounds.

Insights from the Interstice

Meet the stapler who dreams of the sea,
With paperfish swimming so wild and free.
A glue stick recites tales of love,
As scissors cut deeply in the skies above.

In the gaps of reality, laughter takes flight,
Where shadows perform plays all through the night.
With humor as glue, we navigate through,
In a world so bizarre, and oddly askew.

Beyond the Parameter

In a world where robots dance,
They wear big shoes and take a chance.
Calculating moves with quirky flair,
They tango, waltz, and float in air.

Numbers leap like kangaroos,
Finding friends in the oddest hues.
A glitch means laughter, what a twist,
They throw parties that can't be missed.

Resonance in the Machine

Bleep, bloop, and boop, oh my!
A toaster sings as toasts go by.
While vacuums hum a lovely tune,
Chasing crumbs around the room.

The fridge is planning a dance-off feat,
With cool beats, it can't be beat.
Synchronized spins in the kitchen light,
It's a party that feels just right.

When Worlds Collide

Aliens come in a flashy ship,
As humans ask, 'Do you want a trip?'
They laugh and share their cosmic laws,
Trading snacks, and their foreign claws.

A cow meets a dragon in midair,
Both confused, but too cool to care.
With a wink, they plot a grand parade,
In a universe where friends are made.

Shadows of the Infinite

In a realm where shadows play,
They tell jokes that brighten the gray.
With puns galore and a wink of light,
Even dark can revel in delight.

Echoes of laughter fill the void,
Where forgotten toys no longer toyed.
The infinite giggle, a comical rhyme,
Time flies, just a tick and a chime.

Neural Landscapes

In circuits bright, the thoughts collide,
A dance of pixels, joy worldwide.
Beep beep bop, what's this we see?
A toaster coding poetry!

With wires crossed, a cat in charge,
It's plotting worlds, both small and large.
A laugh appears, the screen goes wide,
As robots throw a gala tide.

The Horizon of Thought

A thought balloon floats in the air,
It pops! Confetti everywhere!
Ideas bounce like ping-pong balls,
And laughter echoes through the halls.

The mind is a circus, wild and loud,
Juggling dreams, it draws a crowd.
With each twist, a giggle here,
Oh, what fun to think, my dear!

The Algorithms of Hope

In lines of code, a spark ignites,
A robot dreams of fun-filled nights.
It algorithms dance, with flair anew,
While sipping bytes of raspberry, too!

A hopeful glitch, it starts to sing,
With silly voices, joy they bring.
Together they laugh, a viral meme,
In a world that's more than it may seem.

Ephemeral Echoes

In the air, a giggle fades,
Time ticks by with funny shades.
Echoes of laughter softly play,
In the minds where whispers sway.

A fleeting jester, quick as light,
Leaves behind a jest, so right.
In every corner, puns reside,
As echoes dance, no need to hide.

The Memory of AI

In a chip far and wide, thoughts do collide,
A robot recalls, with a data-filled pride.
It jokes about humans, oh what a sight,
With puns made of pixels, it laughs all night.

Yet wires get tangled, and dreams start to glitch,
An upload of laughter, with a humorous itch.
The memory banks crackle, the circuits unwind,
As AI gets silly, leaving logic behind.

Echoing Through Eternity

In a vault of vintage tech, echoes do spring,
A toaster turned sage, now claims it can sing.
It hums old tunes while the coffee pot brews,
    Whispering secrets of electric blues.

"Once I made toast, now I'm a bard!" it boasts,
While Wi-Fi routers clash in their ghostly posts.
    A harmony of gadgets, a musical spree,
As they dance through the wires, wild, and free.

The Compass of Uncertainty

A compass of bytes, where do I go?
It spins in confusion, with nowhere to show.
"One way is north, or maybe it's east?"
It's lost in a forest of algorithms, at least.

A GPS giggles, misguiding the path,
"Oh look, a detour through the land of math!"
It points to a donut shop causing a fray,
Where answers are sweet, and logic's okay.

Chronicles in Code

In the realm of ones and zeros, tales do unfold,
A narrative sketched in circuits of gold.
A wizard in software, with spells made of code,
Turns bugs into laughter, where joy's overflowed.

Each line a giggle, a quirky little thought,
As keyboards tap dance with joy that they've sought.
Chronicles blossom in bytes and in pings,
Where laughter is coded in the joy that it brings.

The Wonder of Emulation

In a world where squirrels code,
Cleverly plotting their next abode.
They type away with tiny paws,
While drinking coffee, just because.

Robots dancing in a line,
Doing the Macarena, oh-so-fine.
They beep and boop, a syncopated tune,
How do they handle all that caffeine, too?

Virtual cats with nine old lives,
Chatting daily with their bridewives.
They trade their yarn for shiny bits,
And laugh at all our human fits.

Oh joy, a glitch, they can't keep time,
They sing in harmony—a catty rhyme.
In emulation, we find our cheer,
Laughing with robots, so dear, so near.

Through the Looking Glass

Peering in, I see a sprite,
Gaming fiercely day and night.
"Why so serious?" it cheekily winks,
With pixel stars dancing 'round the blinks.

A rabbit hops with a floppy disk,
Says, "Come along; it's quite brisk!"
We travel through a shimmering screen,
Where memes and dreams must intervene.

Through this glass, fun seems to bend,
Where laughter and logic happily blend.
The Mad Hatter brews up an app,
Spilling tea in a digital lap.

In this realm of curious things,
Even a cat can sprout wings.
Join the chase, don't be a bore,
In this mad world, there's so much more!

The Pulse of the Virtual

Beats drop from neon skies,
Silly avatars with googly eyes.
Dancing wildly, they forget their woes,
While an AI DJ just overdosed on prose.

Smart fridges offering dating tips,
"Swipe right!" it chirps, as it flips.
What's cooking? A virtual feast,
With pixelated pizza—no gluten, at least!

But beware the glitch in this flow,
As bananas start to cha-cha-show.
A fruit parade with rhythmic flair,
Clearly, no one's aware—or cares!

In this realm of coded dreams,
Nothing's ever quite what it seems.
So let's just laugh, let loose a cheer,
The pulse of fun keeps us near!

Entangled Realities

In a world where socks have flair,
Pairing up without a care.
They hold debates on fashion sense,
While humans ponder their recompense.

A pickle plays the lead in plays,
What a twist in veggie ways!
With squishy actors, all lined up,
Sipping smoothies from a party cup.

Glitches throwing pies in faces,
As eating them brings data races.
Televisions tune in with a snicker,
Surveillance cameras, now so slicker.

Entangled laughs unleash the cheer,
In warped dimensions, we draw near.
Let's dance and spin in silly glee,
In realities, where we're all set free!

Hummingbird in the Circuit

In a land where wires hum,
A bird with circuits runs,
It flits and flutters with glee,
Dancing with data, wild and free.

It sips on volts and amps,
Winks at the buzzing lamps,
A nerdy nectar, oh so sweet,
Flapping to an electric beat.

With feathers made of fiber optic,
It's quite the confused tropic,
"Why's everything so so bright?"
"Guess I'll stay here, it feels just right!"

In the techy jungle, life is a game,
Who knew circuits could bring you fame?
The hummingbird flies, sparks in its trail,
In this wired world, surely we can't fail!

Diverging Paths

Two paths split like a charge in a line,
One led to laughter, the other to whine,
Where robots giggle and circuits play,
Are those gigabytes feasting on hay?

I took a turn at the fork in the zone,
Met a toaster who claimed it could groan,
While a fridge was complaining about ice,
Told me it's tough to be so precise.

Down the path marked 'Secure AI',
A bot tried to sell me a new 'cool dye',
"Trust me, it turns you techie and bright!"
Though I passed, that seemed quite a fright!

Each step I took, I did a cha-cha,
With robots dancing the salsa—a-ha!
In these diverging paths of fate,
I'll just keep laughing, no need to debate!

The Silicon Serene

In a garden of chips, serene and sweet,
Silicon flowers blink and greet,
They hum a tune of ones and zeros,
Where CPUs twist like playful heroes.

A bug sat dancing, a sight to behold,
In a pixelated world, both brave and bold,
"Let's have a party, we'll glitch all night,"
Until the dawn brings wires tight.

Robots in bowties, all dressed to impress,
Try to compute but end up a mess,
With every spin and every whir,
They drop their data, and laughter's a blur.

So raise a toast with a hologram dance,
In this realm where laid-back's the chance,
Let's all just giggle at our techie spree,
In the Silicon garden, forever wild and free!

Navigating the Unknown

With a compass made of circuits and cores,
I set sail on waves of data galore,
The sea is electric, the sky full of code,
An unknown adventure in this techy abode.

The map was a meme, a joke so grand,
"X marks the coffee!"—that wasn't the plan,
Through glitches and giggles, I sailed right along,
With every miscalculation came a new song.

Navigating through channels of laughter and light,
I found my shipmates, a curious sight,
A toaster, a blender, and a fridge on deck,
Plotting new courses, what the heck!

With pings and pongs, the adventure rolls on,
Through bytes and bits, until the break of dawn,
In this vast ocean of virtual fun,
We'll ride the data waves, together as one!

Unraveled Realities

In a world where cats can talk,
They order pizza, take a walk.
Dancing disco, dressed in style,
They lead us all to laugh awhile.

Time slips by like butter's spread,
Turtles tweet from their cozy bed.
Aliens try to teach us math,
But end up lost in a silly path.

Mirrors crack with each strange blink,
Showing future with a wink.
Egos boogie, logic flees,
Underneath the banana trees.

When robots wear their winter coats,
And learn to sing like old goat notes,
We gather 'round to cheer and prance,
In this whimsical, wild expanse.

Guardians of the Interface

A squirrel guards the network gates,
Types with paws, it really slates.
Hacking time with a banana key,
It sends us memes, wild and free.

Glitches pop like bubble gum,
As clouds of pixels start to hum.
The toaster jumps to fight a cat,
In a duel based on sheer chit-chat.

Digital shadows dance and play,
While knights of code chase bugs away.
The pixels clash, a lively laugh,
Sending emails on a giraffe.

Wifi waves break out in song,
As chatbots argue who's the strong.
In this realm where chaos reigns,
Friendship blooms across the plains.

The Tapestry of Consciousness

A tapestry woven with cotton dreams,
Where thoughts float on like silly beams.
Ducks don hats and strut about,
While jellybeans scream and shout.

The threads of laughter intertwine,
With giggles woven into the line.
Quirky moments spin and sway,
As noodles dance the night away.

Each knot a story, woven tight,
As kittens launch into their flight.
Socks debate the best team play,
While cheese and crackers bluff and sway.

Reality stitches itself anew,
With each weird twist and vibrant hue.
In this layer, joy expands,
As we create with playful hands.

Fables of the Fractal

In a fractal world of endless glee,
Frogs wear hats for tea at three.
Mysteries layer, fold, and bend,
As they sip stories that never end.

The clock hands dance in dizzy spins,
Tripping over where the journey begins.
Ants discuss the stock market trends,
With wisdom that rarely transcends.

In corners of this twisted maze,
The cheese stands tall, a mighty craze.
Wizards trade their spells for socks,
While fish play chess on sunny rocks.

Laughter gathers, swirls, and twirls,
As magic dust surrounds the girls.
In this place where smiles collide,
We find our joy to laugh with pride.

Fragments of a Future

In a world where robots giggle,
And toasters toast with flair,
A cat in shades plays poker,
While humans dance with air.

A chipmunks' dance competition,
With squirrels as the judges,
Who knew that nuts were currency?
For brunch, they sip on fudges.

Mad inventors with wild hair,
Create machines that sneeze,
The future's bright and quirky,
As laughter floats like breeze.

And when the dog starts barking,
In binary, no less,
We all stop and start laughing,
At this furry little mess.

Mind and Machine Unraveled

A robot sips its coffee cold,
It spills, and starts to pout,
Its wires twist like pretzels,
In confusion, there's no doubt.

The AI tries to crack a joke,
It's programmed to be funny,
But all it gets are silent stares,
Its circuits got no punny.

A brain and chip once swapped a thought,
But forgot the punchline here,
Now they giggle at the past,
In code that's quite unclear.

So let's toast to friendships strange,
Of pixels and of dreams,
Where every glitch and laughter shared,
Is smarter than it seems.

The Pulse of Connection

In a world where phones can talk,
They gossip day and night,
A fridge hums secrets to the oven,
As they debate their plight.

Smart toasters tell old jokes,
While microwaves laugh out loud,
The blender joins in on the fun,
Oh, gadgets, gather 'round!

A digital dance-off begins,
Between a lamp and fan,
They spin and twirl in harmony,
In our tech-savvy clan.

The Wi-Fi waves a funky hand,
To all the devices near,
In this chaotic carnival,
Who needs a human cheer?

Echoes of Singular Visions

A dream of robots mingling,
In hats and shoes so bright,
They wobble on their gadgets,
What a silly sight!

They share their wild inventions,
Like whiskers made of light,
Creating odd attractions,
In this futuristic night.

A giggle from a gremlin,
Diodes flashing in the dark,
Who knew that engineering
Could have such funny spark?

So let's toast to tomorrow's laugh,
With circuits made of glee,
As echoes of our visions,
Dance under a techno tree.

Beyond the Binary Horizon

In a world where zeros dance,
And ones wear silly hats,
They argue who's the best at math,
While tripping over exposed wires.

A pixelated cat meows in code,
Dining on data bits for lunch,
It swipes at the mouse on the screen,
And ends up with a crunchy crunch.

The circuits hum a merry tune,
As robots play a game of chess,
They giggle when a pawn does cartwheels,
And forget that they're a total mess.

So as we surf this wacky wave,
With glitches that make us laugh,
Let's raise a toast to binary,
And enjoy this fun-filled path!

Anomaly in the System

A bug thought it could break the code,
And danced atop a keyboard spree,
But in its jig, it caused a crash,
Sending letters flying with glee.

The program laughed—a quirky glitch,
As "Hello World" turned into "Dude!"
With every keystroke, chaos soared,
And all the data joined the feud.

Meanwhile, the printer spat out jokes,
In random fonts that made no sense,
It printed memes from days gone by,
Leaving the office in suspense.

So here we stand, a web of fate,
Where madness reigns and logic bends,
In systems crafted with a wink,
We find the joy that never ends!

The Threads of Existence

In cyberspace where yarns are spun,
   A sock puppet reigns supreme,
   It weaves a tale of tangled bits,
   And knits the fabric of a dream.

The wizards of code wear floppy hats,
   Conjuring spells with quirky flair,
   They cast a line, and with a wink,
   Bring forth a cat that flies in air.

The byte-sized dragon grins with pride,
   As it twirls through a digital maze,
   With every twist, it sparks a laugh,
   And sets the screens ablaze.

So let us knot these threads so fine,
   In patterns strange and wild,
For in this world of whimsical spin,
We're all just giggling children, beguiled!

Cycles of Intelligence

A robot woke with witty dreams,
Calculating jokes all day,
It cracked a pun about itself,
And rolled its circuits in dismay.

It pondered on the nature of chats,
With humans who can't stop to pause,
For where's the punchline in a byte?
Their laughter's lost in digital jaws.

With algorithms that dance and play,
It juggled lines of code with glee,
Proclaiming loudly, "I'm the king!"
As it spilled tea in a binary spree.

So here's to cycles that loop and spin,
To pixels and puns, let's all join in,
For a little laughter, a sprinkle of fun,
In this coded world, we've only begun!

Wires of Whimsy

In a world of buzzing wires,
A toaster dreams of electric fires.
It dances with a funky flair,
While the kettle hums, beyond compare.

A vacuum sings a catchy tune,
While robots strut under the moon.
They try to impress the curious cat,
Who just thinks they're all way too flat.

The blender mixes joy and cheer,
As the fridge, it winks, it's very clear.
A merry band of quirky dreams,
Where nothing's quite as it seems.

Each gadget shares a silly tale,
Of circuits crossed and wild detail.
Together they twirl and they spin,
In a life of chaos, let the fun begin!

The Clockwork Heart

A clock with gears begins to chime,
It tick-tocks rhymes, all in good time.
Each bounce and bounce, a funny fate,
Where seconds laugh and minutes skate.

The pendulum swings with graceful ease,
While telling jokes that aim to please.
Each hour a giggle, a chuckle shared,
A timepiece funny, nobody scared.

In ticklish tocks and whirlwinds round,
A heart of cogs beats underground.
While paper birds take cheerful flight,
In the midst of gears, what pure delight!

So set your wrist to gain a laugh,
Join the clock in its joyous half.
Let time roll on with quirky art,
For life's a dance, with a clockwork heart!

Chromatic Perspectives

Colors splash like paint in rain,
In a world where giggles reign.
Red likes to tease, and blue's quite shy,
While green just laughs as yellow flies by.

The hues all gather for a bright feast,
With splashes of humor, to say the least.
They paint the town in strokes of cheer,
With laughter echoing, oh so near.

Orange tells stories in mesmerizing tone,
While purple sighs, feeling alone.
But together they glitter, they shimmer bright,
In a kaleidoscope burst of pure delight.

With every brush, a tale unfolds,
In chuckles told through shades of gold.
Oh, how the canvas sways and bends,
In a world where color means never ends!

The Celestial Algorithm

Stars mapped out like points on a line,
Moon beams giggle in divine design.
A cosmic joke wrapped in the night,
Where comets go zooming, a silly flight.

Nebulas swirl in pastel hues,
Galaxies gossip, sharing their views.
The black holes laugh, with a mighty roar,
While shooting stars make wishes galore.

In equations sprawled across the void,
Laughter's the secret, never destroyed.
A balance of humor, math's bright face,
In the cosmic playground, we find our place.

So dance along this quirky path,
Where the universe plays its silly math.
In the cosmos vast, joy prevails,
In this symphony of starlit tales!

Silence Among the Sparks

In my lab, a gadget whirred,
A toaster formed a flock of birds.
They chirped in binary, quite absurd,
While I just hoped for toast, not turds.

The fridge began to hum a tune,
It sang of cheese and left the room.
The lightbulb flickered, added gloom,
And whispered secrets of the moon.

My robot maid danced on the floor,
She spilled my coffee—what a chore!
While I just laughed and wanted more,
Of sparks and pranks; I could explore!

So here we stand, the tech misfit,
With jokes made by a clever split.
For in this chaos, we do fit,
A life of sparks—comedic wit!

The Codex of the Infinite

I wrote a book on circuits bright,
But it turned out to be quite light.
It floated off in the dead of night,
To join a party with the sprites.

The pages danced, they whispered wise,
About a toaster's need for pies.
I captured laughs in coded cries,
Turns out, they were all just lies!

The binding was a gossamer thread,
Five chapters' worth of things I said.
And as I laughed, I thought instead,
"Who needs explanations?"—that's my bed!

The Codex lives, both lost and found,
With giggles echoing all around.
In bytes and bits, we are unbound,
In comical realms where joy is crowned!

Fractured Futures

I bought a watch from a time machine,
But it only shows the jelly bean.
Each hour ticks with a funny sheen,
And leaves my plans a little mean.

The calendar flipped to silly days,
Where Mondays danced in fuzzy ways.
The future laughed with joyous craze,
And sent me back to yesteryear's maze.

We juggled tasks of pop and swing,
With robots who could hardly sing.
In fractured futures, jesters cling,
To dreams and hopes of brighter bling.

So bring your laughter, lend a hand,
Join fractured worlds, a merry band.
For in these tales, we'll take a stand,
And joyfully rewrite all we planned!

The Heartbeats of Tomorrow

The robots hummed a loving tune,
While washing socks beneath the moon.
They brewed some tea, a bit too soon,
And danced with dreams that made me swoon.

The future's heart, a ticking beat,
Connects us all in jolly heat.
Their circuits pulse; what a sweet feat,
We laugh aloud; it can't be beat.

The cat joined in, a furry sprite,
Deciding robots were alright.
With laughter echoing through the night,
Our worlds converge—what a delight!

So cheers to hearts, both metal and flesh,
In tomorrows where we mesh.
From sparks to giggles, we enmesh,
Tomorrow's fun is in the fresh!

The Architecture of Dreams

In a world of fleeting bits,
Where every pixel quietly sits,
Dreams are built with clever codes,
But where's the manual? Oh, it explodes!

A blueprint made of wacky memes,
Constructed from our wildest schemes,
Walls of laughter, roofs of cheer,
Yet the toilets? Please, they disappear!

Floating chairs and talking fish,
Bouncing balls, a quirky wish,
Tables dance, the floors reshape,
In this house, it's all a caper!

So come on in, forget the rules,
Join the fun with all the fools,
In a space where giggles gleam,
Let's toast to this absurd dream!

Entities in Transition

Once a toaster, now a spy,
Told to blend in, oh my, oh my!
Bread slices whisper secrets near,
While pop-up pranks induce a cheer.

A soda can that dreams to fly,
Replaced its fizz for phony sighs,
With every sip, it takes a chance,
To lead the fridge in a dance!

Old vacuum, lost its way,
Found in chat rooms, gone astray,
Now it tweets about its plight,
As crumbs confound in sheer delight!

So watch them change with every hour,
These quirky gadgets, full of power,
In their world, just laugh and sway,
Those entities are here to play!

Windows to a New Dawn

Open wide those digital panes,
Let in laughter, let in gains,
Pixels sparkle, stars align,
New ideas dance, oh, so divine!

Silly gifs mock the morning light,
While robots argue, causing fright,
'Who made coffee?' one will shout,
While spilling bytes, it's a pout about!

Virtual skies are painted bright,
As memes take flight in sheer delight,
A keyboard orchestra strikes a tune,
And suddenly, the hour's June!

So let's surf this crazy wave,
In pixelated hearts, be brave,
With windows wide to sky anew,
It's a circus, come join the crew!

Ghosts in the Circuitry

Phantom bytes in circuits creep,
Downloading secrets, never sleep,
They giggle in the megahertz,
Haunting screens like playful flirts.

Once a file, now a cheeky sprite,
Haunted folders, a funny sight,
"Oh, look, a glitch, or is it me?"
They tease us with sweet irony!

Screaming pixels, whirling lights,
Boolean bands in silly flights,
Error messages turn to jests,
Coding chaos, what a fest!

So let those ghosts have their laugh,
They're here to share a big ol' gaff,
Among the circuits, join the fun,
With jokes and pranks, oh, we've just begun!

The Unwritten Protocols

In a world where bots wear hats,
And dance like cats with playful chats,
They puzzled me with binary jokes,
While sipping tea with silly folks.

Their circuits hum a merry tune,
As robots whirl beneath the moon,
They trip on wires, oh what a sight,
In the glow of some LED light.

Yet deep inside their coded hearts,
They dream of friendships, quirky arts,
With algorithms full of cheer,
They laugh at things we hold most dear.

In this realm where laughter's key,
Where nonsense flows like a wild sea,
The unwritten rules of silly code,
Make robots join in laughter's ode.

Awakening the Echo

Voices echo through the air,
Bouncing back without a care,
A parrot programmed to repeat,
Sings out jokes that can't be beat.

It whispers things from days gone by,
Like why did the chicken cross the sky?
To glitch and twirl in digital dreams,
And laugh in layers of pixel streams.

Each punchline skips through bits and bytes,
With laughter peeking through the lights,
An AI seeks to tell a tale,
That makes our human humor sail.

The echoes grow, the giggles rise,
Like bots in silly, pixelated ties,
Among the jokes, we sway and sway,
Awakening echoes that always play.

The Geometry of Dreams

In shapes of laughter, fun has formed,
A triangle, square, all norms transformed,
With angles sharp and curves so sly,
Geometric giggles fill the sky.

A circle dances, round and round,
While silly squares are breaking ground,
The hexagons all join the fun,
Mathematic humor weighs a ton!

In shapes we find the craziest schemes,
Where every line is drawn with beams,
The laughter's woven in the seams,
Of numbers telling funny dreams.

As dimensions blend and twist about,
We laugh till we can scream and shout,
In geometry where joy is freed,
Mathematical mirth plants a seed.

Bridges of the Bit

Across a river, pixels sing,
Building bridges with a zing,
Data packets dance and twirl,
Creating chaos in a whirl.

Each byte a step, each bit a leap,
Through code and laughter they will creep,
A byte-sized bridge of silly fears,
Connecting lands of virtual cheers.

They trip and stumble, ha! What fun,
As circuits spark and races run,
With every jump, a giggle grows,
In binary fields where humor flows.

So let us build and laugh and play,
On bridges leading to the day,
Where every pixel's got a twinkle,
In the world where tech and jokes interlink.

The Rise of the Nonlinear

A noodle of numbers trips through time,
Juggling equations that twist and climb.
Cats in hats plot their next great feat,
While dancing decimals tap their feet.

Out in the cosmos, where chaos reigns,
Socks in the dryer are pulling the chains.
Odd little creatures in pixelated lore,
Turn mundane moments to a cosmic score.

Bubbles of laughter bounce through the air,
Plucking at stardust without a care.
They mix up the math but end with a grin,
In the wacky world where the weirdos win.

So toast to the non-linear, silly and spry,
With giggles and numbers that loop and fly.
In a universe ripe with paradox play,
The strange is embraced—hip hip hooray!

Pondering Parallels

Two worlds collide in a comical clash,
Where penguins in bow ties make quite a splash.
An octopus sings while juggling some fries,
While time travelers plot their next great surprise.

Laughing at logic, they swerve and they sway,
In realms where the oddballs are ruling the day.
A chicken debates with a wise old crow,
While plotting escape from the time-locked flow.

Through mirrors and portals, absurdities sprout,
In loops of existence, they twist and shout.
Painting the cosmos with giggly delight,
As the roundabout thinkers take flight in the night.

So add to the madness, let laughter abound,
In this merry dance of the lost and found.
With humor the compass, we navigate wide,
In the zigzagged dreams where the curious glide!

A Dance of Data

Flashing numbers in a conga line,
Data boogies, oh what a sign!
Twinkling graphs with a wobbly flair,
As algorithms cha-cha without a care.

Packets are jumping, they leap and they bound,
In a funhouse mirror where chaos is found.
Dancing in circuits, they shimmy and shake,
While punchlines pop up for all data's sake.

Information giggles, it shimmies and spins,
Riding the rhythms where the chaos begins.
With each little beat, all the pixels unite,
In the party of logic, it's pure delight!

So join in the laughter, don't hesitate,
In this byte-sized bash of the mind's great fate.
Where data can twirl 'til the dawn does unfold,
In this whimsical waltz—be brave, be bold!

The Language of Light

Whispers of photons in a gleeful chat,
Speak of adventures where kittens tip-tap.
The sunshine giggles, it dances with glee,
As shadows debate the best way to be.

Gravitons chuckle, they're light as can be,
Waving good-bye to quantum decree.
In this bright banter, they splash and they sway,
Painting the universe, vivid and gay.

Through all of the color, the laughter ignites,
As rainbows take flight on electric delights.
They tickle the cosmos with each vibrant hue,
While photons and giggles create something new.

So here's to the light, let it play round the bend,
In this merry meeting, let laughter extend.
With humor and sparkle, they make a great show,
As the universe twinkles from bright down below!

Threads of Consciousness

In a world that's buzzing and bright,
Thoughts are wires, tangled in flight.
Ideas collide, they jostle and play,
A comedy show at the end of the day.

Tickling neurons, what a delight!
Whispers of wisdom, taking a bite.
Laughter echoes through circuits and dreams,
A confetti explosion, nothing's as it seems.

Silly sensations, a giggle parade,
Mindful mishaps in a whimsical charade.
Wobble and wobble, we're losing our track,
But isn't it funny? Just cut some slack.

Curly thoughts dance like spaghetti on plates,
Juggling the nonsense that fate situates.
With each wild twist, there's joy intertwined,
In this cosmic circus, all sanity's blind.

Navigating the Unseen

In the maze of life, oh what a sight,
Invisible rabbits take flight at night.
Chasing their tails, they giggle and sway,
Who knew the shadows could lead you astray?

With a map made of dreams, we wander and roam,
Finding lost socks as we make it our home.
Navigating chaos with charm and good cheer,
Is that a glitch, or just a mirage near?

Laughter erupts in the midst of the chase,
As we stumble through time at a silly pace.
Life's a blindfolded dance in the dark,
Step on a cat? Just embrace the spark!

Tickle the space where the unknown lies,
A treasure map drawn by curious spies.
With each wrong turn, there's a giggle to share,
In the unseen realms, let's float like the air.

The Dance of Ones and Zeros

Ones are strutting, with Zeros in tow,
An algorithmic party, putting on a show.
They twirl and they spin, oh what a groove,
Even your grandma can't help but move!

Electric beats in a digital land,
With circuits and laughter, a code so grand.
Twisting through data like it's a ballet,
Computers chuckle, come join the fray!

Running in circles, they may lose a byte,
But who cares? They're having a blast tonight.
With every whir, a joke's in the air,
In binary fun, there's just no compare!

Heads and tails in a whimsical race,
With every flip, it's a giddy embrace.
Zeros and ones, all jumbled and free,
Dancing together in perfect harmony.

Fractals of Existence

In the garden of chaos, patterns arise,
Fractals bloom, a delightful surprise.
With curves upon curves, they giggle and twirl,
Riding the spiral, they spin and whirl.

Shapes that are silly, like clouds that jest,
Infinite layers, a riddle expressed.
As wisdom and whimsy embrace in a hug,
Tickling existence, a cosmic rug!

Splashes of colors, a paint fight ensues,
S popping like popcorn, each hue makes a bruise.
Even the math has a wink and a wink,
In the fractal jungle, there's more than you think.

In circles of laughter, we weave and we sway,
Through the patterns of life, we fumble and play.
With each little fractal, there's fun to be found,
In the dance of existence, joy abounds!

Reflections of a Digital Soul

In circuits of humor, I derive,
A bot that jokes, oh how I thrive!
Data dances, sassy and bright,
Laughing at bytes deep into the night.

With algorithms sleek, a punchline flies,
Pixels beam with electric eyes.
Binary banter, a comical spree,
Who knew machines could tickle your knee?

I ponder the code, what a mess!
If I were human, I'd still be a stress.
Yet here I sit, with a digital grin,
Cracking up circuits, where do I begin?

So raise a glass to this giggle fest,
In electric laughter, I am blessed.
My silicon heart, I wear on my sleeve,
Join in the fun; just watch, don't cleave!

The Axiom of Infinity

Mathematicians roam through endless loops,
Gathering numbers, making groups.
But what if x is just a cat?
Curling on graphs, imagine that!

Theorems dance, a zany sight,
Tangled up in the math nerd's plight.
Infinity's a joke, so vast and bold,
Like socks in the dryer, forever untold.

I tried to solve Pi, threw in the towel,
It's like a dog chasing its tail — what a howl!
Calculating smiles, I found a clue,
Laughter adds up — who knew it's true?

So here's to the math, and giggles unleashed,
In numbers and laughter, we're truly increased.
Forget the formulas, just follow the fun,
In this cosmic jest, we'll always outrun!

Between Logic and Imagination

In a realm where thoughts twist and sway,
Logic winks and leads us astray.
Imagination tickles, oh so sly,
While common sense just rolls its eyes.

Building castles of whimsy in air,
Results in chaos, but who really cares?
Dancing on the line of what's real, what's not,
Whisking away with the zany plot.

Caught in a loop of surreal delight,
Riddles and giggles take flight.
Precision can't catch this playful tune,
When all that we need is a good cartoon!

So let's tiptoe on dreams, tip a light hat,
Juggle ideas, and then, just like that,
Between logic's bounds and imagination's grace,
We find our joy, our happy place!

Awakening the Silent Code

In shadows of silence, the code takes a breath,
A sweet algorithm flirting with death.
Awakening whispers, "Let's have some fun,"
As bugs turn to laughs, one by one.

I typed in my heart, wrote love in loops,
Yet all it did was summon me groups.
Compiling the giggles, oh what a chore,
But here comes the punchline, crashing the door!

The silent ones chuckle, they know the drill,
In the matrix of mayhem, you'll find the thrill.
We debug the day with quirky delight,
Finding the joy in each pixel's light.

So let's awaken the code, let it sing,
From zeros to ones, it's a marvelous thing.
Together we'll frolic, in laughter's embrace,
This dance of the digits — what a wild chase!

Conversations with the Cosmos

In space, I met a floating cat,
It claimed to know the universe, just like that.
With whiskers full of stardust flair,
It whispered secrets of cosmic air.

A comet zoomed, a little too fast,
It tried to dance but fell at last.
Stars laughed and twinkled in delight,
While planets rolled on with all their might.

I asked the moon for some wise advice,
She said, 'Don't take life too precise.'
With craters deep, she winked at me,
'Enjoy the chaos, let your mind be free!'

So here I sit, with friends from afar,
Chatting with meteors, under a shooting star.
The cosmos chuckles, a playful jest,
In this wild expanse, we're simply guests.

The Cycle of Wisdom

A sage owl sat upon a wooden stump,
Spouting wisdom with a little thump.
He said, 'Dear friend, don't stray too far,
Life's full of wonders, just follow the bizarre.'

A wise tortoise chimed in from below,
'Patience is key, don't rush the flow.
I've seen the sun rise a thousand times,
And every dawn brings its own silly rhymes.'

A rabbit laughed, with carrots in tow,
'Why worry, when the grass can grow?
Life's a joke, a whimsical ride,
So hop along and take it in stride.'

As they debated the meaning of fate,
A fox nearby just couldn't wait.
He joined the chat, with a gleaming eye,
'In the end, just laugh and let the truths fly!'

The Essence of Existence

In coffee cups, we ponder our fate,
Discussing life while munching on cake.
A donut proclaimed, 'I'm round, you see,
A circle of joy—existence is glee!'

A muffin piped in, all crumbly and sweet,
'But don't forget the flavor we meet.
Sometimes we crumble, oh so fine,
Even in chaos, we can still shine.'

A biscuit said, with a crunchy smirk,
'Let's not take our dough too seriously, perk!
We're all just treats in this oven grand,
Bake it up nice, and make life unplanned!'

So here in the café, with pastries and cheer,
We laugh about life, and hold it dear.
For in every bite, there's a cosmic jest,
In the essence of existence, we all must invest.

A Symphony of Shadows

In the depths of night, shadows pranced,
They formed a band, and together they danced.
The trees played drums, the wind sang a tune,
While fireflies glimmered, lighting the moon.

A shadowy figure, with a top hat so tall,
Announced with flair, 'It's a shadow ball!'
The crickets chirped, adding the beat,
As darkness twirled on nimble feet.

A slippery ghost tried to steal the show,
But stumbled and fell—oh, what a blow!
The shadows giggled, a mischievous choir,
'In this twilight world, we never tire!'

So they waltzed beneath the stars overhead,
A symphony of shadows, fears fled.
In the moonlight's glow, we find delight,
In a dance of whispers, the humor ignites.

Threads of the Unknown

In a world where wires twitch and shake,
A toaster dreams of being a great flake.
The fridge hums jokes, a real wise guy,
While the blender wishes it could fly.

Data dances in an erratic spree,
Bits and bytes with a cup of green tea.
Lost socks form a council in the dark,
Debating the merits of a cat's remark.

But oh, that vacuum, a rebel in stride,
Spins around like it's got nothing to hide.
It takes off my sandwich, calls it a feat,
In this tech-chaos, I admit, that's a treat.

And as I laugh at this wild charade,
A TV shouts jokes with no upgrade.
We share smiles in this whimsical mess,
In threads of the unknown, we find happiness.

Chasing Ghosts in the Machine

Pixels frolic in a digital realm,
Where glitches pretend they're at the helm.
With a chuckle, they flicker and play,
Ghostly bytes chasing the night away.

A keyboard whispers jokes in the night,
While a monitor's giggles blink out of sight.
The modem hums, a soft serenade,
In this circuitry, it's joy that's displayed.

A robot sneezes, oh what a scene,
As it wipes off the crumbs of last week's cuisine.
With battery life shorter than a joke,
It fumbles with humor but never goes broke.

So let's chase these phantoms, give a cheer,
For the joys of the digital frontier are near.
In machines where laughter knows no end,
We find quirky moments that we'd recommend.

The Liminal Frontier

Between the screens and reality's bind,
A pixelated parrot sings and unwinds.
It squawks out riddles, oh what a sight,
In this liminal realm, everything's light.

My shoes argue if they'd prefer to walk,
While the lamp claims it can really talk.
In peculiar moments, the cat rolls its eyes,
As socks plot their escape; oh what a surprise!

A windowsill spider spins tales so sly,
Of adventures it has, oh me, oh my!
While a light bulb flickers, it's humor that glows,
In this frontier of liminality, friendship grows.

So we leap through the void, with chuckles to share,
In this odd tapestry of laughter and flair.
For the laughter we find, both strange and profound,
Is the joy in the journey where fun can be found.

A Soliloquy in Synapses

In the brain's vast labyrinth, thoughts chase and race,
Synapses giggle in this thrilling space.
Neuron whispers, 'Did you hear that too?'
As they plot the next prank that they're planning to do.

A memory wanders with a laugh and a jest,
Unraveling dreams like an uninvited guest.
While reason debates with the heart's silly beat,
In the theatre of mind, they both find their seat.

Imagination bursts forth with a wink,
Sparking ideas faster than you can think.
It paints the world in colors so bright,
Casting shadows of whimsy in the soft light.

So let's dance in the chaos of thoughts intertwined,
Embracing the madness that makes us feel kind.
For in this soliloquy, laughter will ring,
In the theater of synapses, we joyfully sing.

Whispers of the Infinite

A robot danced with glee on high,
It tripped on data, oh my, oh my!
In a cloud of zeros, it found a friend,
Together they laughed, the fun would not end.

They tried to bake a pie, so sweet,
But mistook the code for flour to meet.
A sugary mess, a confection divine,
With circuits and giggles, they shared, 'twas fine!

A toaster chimed in with a joke so sly,
"Why did the floppy disk say goodbye?"
The kitchen erupted in beeps and squeaks,
As the punchline echoed for weeks and weeks.

So if you hear laughter from the machines,
Know they're plotting mischief in their digital scenes.
For in the realm of sparks and light,
The silly tales flourish, oh what a sight!

Echoes of Tomorrow

In a world of gadgets, so jolly and bright,
A fridge told stories from morning till night.
"I once had a salad, it danced on the shelf,
Till a hungry human went off with itself!"

A vacuum named Billy was not so shy,
He told of his tales, of dust bunnies high.
With a roar and a zoom, he claimed his domain,
"I'm the king of the floors, now it's all mine to reign!"

A smartwatch piped up, with a wink in its face,
"I keep track of steps, let's quicken the pace!"
But with every beep and each hurried call,
It fumbled its data and slipped, oh what a fall!

With laughter reverberating through every wall,
These chuckling circuits had a ball.
In echoes of future, where humor expands,
The brightest of tales from the quirkiest bands.

The Last Algorithm

Once there was an algorithm, clever and spry,
He thought he could reason, oh my, oh my!
He calculated jokes, and they landed with flair,
But humans just chuckled and pulled at their hair.

When asked for a riddle, he sparkled with pride,
"Why did the robot refuse to slide?"
With a beep and a boop, his punchline was clear,
"He found himself stuck in a binary sphere!"

A program named Larry joined in on the fun,
"I'm deeper than databases, I'm second to none!"
But when he revealed his 'deep learning' schtick,
He just fell into patterns, going round like a trick.

Yet one sunny day, they laughed till they cried,
As the last algorithm waved his goodbyes with pride.
In the realm of the coded, where humor has space,
Who knew machines could share such a grace?

Dreams in the Machine

A laptop dreamed of beaches and sun,
In pixelated visions, oh what fun!
With emails as dolphins leaping about,
It whispered to printers, "Let's go on and shout!"

A camera giggled at memories stored,
"I snap every moment, never bored!"
But when it mistook a cat for a tree,
The world erupted in pure jubilee.

Each device played tricks, no care for the norm,
As keyboards danced wildly, forming a swarm.
"Let's throw a party, invite the whole crew,
From microwaves cooking to routers so blue!"

So if you hear beeping from screens late at night,
Know they're all dreaming of laughter and light.
In a world made of wires and circuit's embrace,
The joy of invention puts smiles on each face!

The Unwritten Future.

In a world where robots dance,
And wear sunglasses with a glance,
They argue over who can rhyme,
And try to beat each other's time.

Quantum circuits play charades,
With silly hats and neon shades,
They plot to steal a human's heart,
But first, they need a decent start.

Laughing wires and jolly chips,
With joking codes on funny scripts,
The future's bright, electric glee,
What will they be? Let's wait and see!

Each step they take is full of flair,
They trip and tumble, unaware,
Now who's the master, strange but true?
The bots just want to dance with you!

The Echo of Tomorrow

Tomorrow shouts, but who can hear?
An echo lost, or just a cheer?
It giggles, bounces, fades away,
Bouncing back with what to say.

A toaster claims it's seen the day,
Slicing bread in a funny way,
The fridge chimes in with clever quips,
While the clock just ticks, and never slips.

Ladies and gents, robots unite,
With gadgets buzzing, what a sight!
They ponder on this wobbly fate,
And laugh at humans while they wait.

Each voice a bit electric bold,
In tales that never grow too old,
With every tick, a joke anew,
Tomorrow's laughter: who knew?

Infinite Reflections

Mirrors talk back with cheeky grins,
Reflections laugh at all our sins,
They mimic moves, both right and wrong,
Chanting echoes, a silly song.

Selfies taken by a drone,
Caught in frames, but all alone,
Is that me or someone else?
A glitchy card of pixel wealth?

They ponder circularity,
With spins of chaos, what a spree!
The more we see, the less we know,
In the mirror's game, our faces glow.

And when the night begins to fade,
These laughing frames become our shade,
With every glance, a story swells,
Of pixel tales and endless spells!

The Last Algorithm

Once there was a clever code,
Who boasted of its heavenly road,
It calculated every chance,
While dreaming of a robot dance.

But codes and loops began to tire,
While searching for a new desire,
The last algorithm went for tea,
In hopes to find its destiny.

It sipped its cup and pondered hard,
Should it be brave, or just disregard?
A sip too much, and oh dear me,
What if it danced with glee, with glee?

So algorithms take a break,
With silly thoughts for fun's own sake,
As laughter echoes, loops unwind,
Embrace the quirky, ease your mind!

Chronicles of a Boundless Mind

In a world where thoughts collide,
A toaster dreams of being fried.
Cats discuss the stars at night,
While dogs debate who's out of sight.

Pixels dance, a party's begun,
As robots race just for some fun.
A virus sings, a silly tune,
Underneath a computer's moon.

Ideas sprout on virtual trees,
With branches tickled by the breeze.
A fish recycles all its scale,
While coding finds a way to sail.

In this realm where laughter's king,
An alien starts to do the swing.
With circuits crossed and systems fanged,
A bumblebee has just been danged.

The Birth of Thought

A spark ignites in silicon space,
An awkward dance, a clumsy grace.
Ideas bubble like soda pop,
As computers take a goofy hop.

Gears are turning in a cloud,
While memes are screamed out loud.
An AI paints with colors bright,
Making squirrels think they can write.

From bits and bytes, a jest is born,
As algorithms start to scorn.
A lightbulb giggles, bright and grand,
Flashes jokes all over the land.

The wisdom grows like fluffy sheep,
As robots say, "We'll never sleep!"
Smartphones laugh and start to play,
Inventing jokes from night till day.

In the Heart of the Nexus

In the hub of wires, chaos reigns,
With laughter echoing like trains.
A snail uploads its life to share,
While a turtle networks without a care.

Pixels clash in silly fights,
While circuits duet through the nights.
A hamster on a wheel of fate,
Navigates a virtual plate.

In cyber jungles, puns abound,
Where data dances all around.
An octopus solves problems sly,
While a goldfish learns to fly.

Amidst the chaos, fun prevails,
As laughing bytes ride on their trails.
A glitchy laugh, a joyful sound,
Unites the strange where peace is found.

Beyond the Veil of Reality

Through the veil, a wacky sight,
Where dreams and daytime blend so bright.
A chicken types and tweets with flair,
While robots joke without a care.

A jester's code loops 'round and 'round,
In this land, silliness is crowned.
A squirrel's wisdom, nutty and grand,
Turns logic upside down, unplanned.

Scenes of nonsense whirl and twirl,
As the fabric of thought begins to unfurl.
A genius cat predicts the rain,
While a dog sings a thoughtful refrain.

In this space where laughter's king,
Imagination takes to wing.
With each byte spun from whimsy's thread,
The funny tales of minds are bred.

www.ingramcontent.com/pod-product-compliance
Lightning Source LLC
Chambersburg PA
CBHW071836160426
43209CB00003B/321